Biodiversity
of Wetlands

GREG PYERS

MACMILLAN
LIBRARY

First published in 2011 by
MACMILLAN EDUCATION AUSTRALIA PTY LTD
15–19 Claremont Street, South Yarra 3141

Visit our website at www.macmillan.com.au or go directly to www.macmillanlibrary.com.au

Associated companies and representatives throughout the world.

National Library of Australia Cataloguing-in-Publication entry

Pyers, Greg.
    Of wetlands / Greg Pyers.
    ISBN: 9781420278866 (hbk.)
    Biodiversity.
    Includes index.
    For primary school age.
    Wetlands—Juvenile literature. Wetland ecology—Juvenile literature.
    Biodiversity conservation—Juvenile literature.

577.68

Publisher: Carmel Heron
Commissioning Editor: Niki Horin
Managing Editor: Vanessa Lanaway
Editor: Georgina Garner
Proofreader: Tim Clarke
Designer: Kerri Wilson
Page layout: Raul Diche
Photo researcher: Wendy Duncan (management: Debbie Gallagher)
Illustrator: Richard Morden
Production Controller: Vanessa Johnson

Printed in China

Acknowledgements
The author and publisher are grateful to the following for permission to reproduce copyright material:

Front cover photograph: Bird life in Kakadu National Park, Australia courtesy of photolibrary/LOOK-foto/Don Fuchs.
Back cover photographs courtesy of Shutterstock/sobur (white heron), /Ladynin (water lily).

Photographs courtesy of:
Corbis/All Canada Photos/Michael Wheatley, **17**, Niall Benvie, **8**, Annie Griffiths Belt, **21**, /Robert Harding World Imagery/Christian
Kober, **23**, Martin Harvey, **25**, /Radius Images, **4**; Dreamstime/Steve Byland, **20**; Getty Images/All Canada Photos/Chris Harris, **7**, /
AFP/Romeo Gacad, **14**, /National Geographic/David Doubilet, **19**, /National Geographic/Nicole Duplaix, **15**, /National Geographic/
Steve Winter, **10**, /Photodisc/Theo Allofs, **27**, /The Image Bank/Ben Cranke, **29**; istockphoto/Torsten Karock, **28**; Newspix, **24**, /Chris
Crerar, **9**, /Sarah Reed, **11**; photolibrary/Peter Arnold Images/Martin Harvey, **13**, /Photo Researchers/Susan Leavines, **16**, /Ticket/Bob
Wickham, **22**; Shutterstock/Tony Wear, **18**. Background and design images used throughout Shutterstock/Raimundas, (bullrushes), /
Frank Anusewicz (lily pads), /Shelley Shay (waterlilies).

While every care has been taken to trace and acknowledge copyright, the publisher tenders their apologies for any accidental
infringement where copyright has proved untraceable. They would be pleased to come to a suitable arrangement with the rightful
owner in each case.

Please note
At the time of printing, the Internet addresses appearing in this book were correct. Owing to the dynamic nature of the Internet,
however, we cannot guarantee that all these addresses will remain correct.

Contents

Glossary words

When a word is printed in **bold**, you can look up its meaning in the Glossary on page 31.

What is biodiversity?

Biodiversity, or biological diversity, describes the variety of living things in a particular place, in a particular **ecosystem** or across the whole Earth.

Measuring biodiversity

The biodiversity of a particular area is measured on three levels:

- **species** diversity, which is the number and variety of species in the area
- genetic diversity, which is the variety of **genes** each species has. Genes determine the characteristics of different living things. A variety of genes within a species enables it to **adapt** to changes in its environment.
- ecosystem diversity, which is the variety of **habitats** in the area. A diverse ecosystem has many habitats within it.

Many species of birds, such as flamingos, are part of the biodiversity of wetlands, such as these wetlands in France.

Species diversity

Some habitats, such as rainforests and wetlands, have very high biodiversity. More than 50 species of ants have been found in 1 square metre of leaf litter in the Amazon Rainforest, in South America. The wetlands of the Lower Mekong Basin in south-east Asia have more than 1300 species of freshwater fish and 160 species of molluscs, such as snails.

Habitats and ecosystems

Wetlands are habitats, which are places where plants and animals live. Within a wetland habitat, there are also many smaller habitats, sometimes called microhabitats. Some wetland microhabitats are the wetland bottom and the wetland edge. Different kinds of **organisms** live in these places. The animals, plants, other living things and non-living things and all the ways they affect each other make up a wetland ecosystem.

Biodiversity under threat

The variety of species on Earth is under threat. There are somewhere between 5 million and 30 million species on Earth. Most of these species are very small and hard to find, so only about 1.75 million species have been described and named. These are called known species.

Scientists estimate that as many as 50 species become **extinct** every day. Extinction is a natural process, but human activities have sped up the rate of extinction by up to 1000 times.

Known species of organisms on Earth

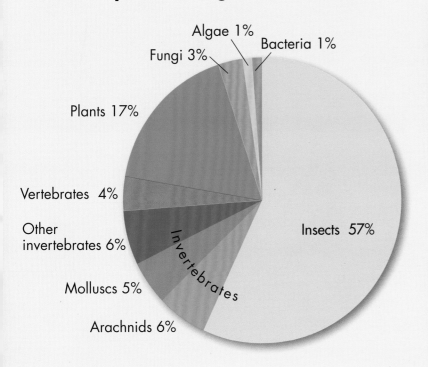

- Algae 1%
- Bacteria 1%
- Fungi 3%
- Plants 17%
- Vertebrates 4%
- Other invertebrates 6%
- Molluscs 5%
- Arachnids 6%
- Insects 57%

Invertebrates

*The known species of organisms on Earth can be divided into bacteria, **algae**, fungi, plant and animal species. Animal species are classified as vertebrates or invertebrates.*

Approximate numbers of known vertebrate species

ANIMAL GROUP	KNOWN SPECIES
Fish	31 000
Birds	10 000
Reptiles	8 800
Amphibians	6 500
Mammals	5 500

Why is biodiversity important?

Biodiversity is important for many reasons. The diverse **organisms** in an **ecosystem** take part in natural processes essential to the survival of all living things. Biodiversity produces food and medicine. It is also important to people's quality of life.

Natural processes

Humans are part of many ecosystems. Our survival depends on the natural processes that go on in ecosystems. Through natural processes, air and water is cleaned, waste is decomposed, **nutrients** are recycled and disease is kept under control. Natural processes depend on the organisms that live in the soil, on the plants that produce oxygen and absorb **carbon dioxide**, and on the organisms that break down dead plants and animals. When **species** of organisms become **extinct**, natural processes may stop working.

Food

We depend on biodiversity for our food. The world's major food plants have all been bred from plants in the wild. Wild plants are important sources of **genes** for breeding new disease-resistant food crops. If wild plants become extinct, their genes are lost.

Environmental benefits

Ecosystems play a huge role in recycling waste, removing **pollutants** from the air and water, and providing other environmental benefits. Scientists have placed a money value on these services to show how important ecosystems are. They estimate that if humans had to do the same work it would cost US$33 trillion a year. About US$4.9 trillion of this value is due to wetland ecosystems.

Did you know?

West African wild rice is a wetland plant that was first cultivated 2000 years ago. Different types of wild rice from other wetlands have also been cultivated. Today, half the world's population depends on rice as a staple food.

Quality of life

Biodiversity is important to people's quality of life. Animals and plants inspire wonder. They are part of our **heritage**. For many people, a walk through a wetland is a pleasant activity that is made even more enjoyable by the wildlife they come across. Seeing animal and plant biodiversity reminds us that we share the world with all manner of life forms, and it can give us a sense of belonging in the world.

Watching wildlife in a wetland is an example of how biodiversity can improve a person's quality of life.

Extinct species

Humans sometimes introduce non-native species into wetland environments, causing the extinction of other species and reducing biodiversity. The Nile perch, a large freshwater fish species, was introduced to Africa's Lake Victoria in the 1950s. It has caused the extinction of hundreds of **endemic species** of fish.

Wetlands of the world

There are several definitions of a wetland. In this book, a wetland is an area that is permanently or temporarily covered in water, not including oceans or seas. Wetlands may have fresh water, salt water or **brackish** water. There are wetlands on all continents.

Freshwater wetlands

Some freshwater wetlands have water all year round, while others dry up for weeks, months or even years at a time. The wetlands may be as small as a room in a house or many thousands of square kilometres in area. There are many different types of freshwater wetlands.

Bogs

Bogs may have very little or no open water at all. They may simply be low-lying areas of waterlogged soil. Bogs are important **habitats** for animals such as frogs.

Lakes

Lakes are large areas of water that are surrounded by land. Some lakes have fresh water, and others are saltwater lakes. Permanent lakes have water year-round, but temporary lakes are dry some of the time.

Swamps or marshes

These wetlands are like shallow lakes, where plants grow in, under and on top of the water. Some swamps or marshes may dry out every summer or during periods of drought. Waterbirds breed in great numbers in these wetlands.

Oxbow lakes

Oxbow lakes, or billabongs, are formed by slow-moving rivers and may be best described as ponds. They often have a higher biodiversity than the rivers that created them. When the river floods, animals that have bred in an oxbow lake are able to move out of the lake.

oxbow lake

oxbow lake

An oxbow lake, or billabong, is a U-shaped pond that is created when part of a river is cut off from the rest of the river.

An estuary is usually a sheltered area, where fresh water from a river and salt water from the sea meet. This aerial image shows the estuary where the Murray River enters the sea, at Goolwa, in South Australia.

Coastal wetlands

Coastal wetlands are influenced by the tides, which go in and out about twice a day. Coastal wetlands are very important breeding grounds for many **species** of marine fish and waterbirds. There are many different types of coastal wetlands.

Salt marshes

Salt marshes are found along the coast, between the low-tide and high-tide marks. Some plants in a salt marsh are heaths and saltbushes. They provide sheltered habitats for many marine and land species.

Mangrove swamps

Mangroves are short trees that grow in the mud between the low-tide and high-tide marks. They provide shelter for many species to breed and they trap **nutrients**, which support the growth of plants and marine animals.

Estuaries

An **estuary** is a body of water where a river meets the sea. They are usually well sheltered from tides and winds, and they are rich in nutrients that were carried by the river. Many species of marine fish breed in estuaries, because of the shelter and the plentiful food.

Wetland biodiversity

Wetlands have very high biodiversity. The availability of water in a wetland means that lush **vegetation** can grow. A wetland with a large variety of plant **species** can support a large variety of animal species.

Wetland plants

Wetland plants provide small **habitats**, called microhabitats, for animals. Different types of plants provide different types of habitats.

Floating pond plants

Plants such as waterlilies and duckweed have leaves that float on the water's surface. They may have roots that grow in the soil at the bottom of the pond or roots that dangle in the water. Floating plants can be platforms for pond animals, such as frogs and damselflies, to rest on. They can also be hiding places for **aquatic** animals escaping from **predators** such as birds.

Submerged pond plants

Submerged plants, such as pondweed and **algae**, grow completely underwater. Pondweeds are important for fish because they add oxygen to the water. Some insects, such as dragonflies, lay their eggs on submerged plants.

Emergent pond plants

Plants such as reeds and rushes grow in the shallows with their stems rising above the surface of the water. Emergent plants provide breeding sites for birds such as reed warblers, which use the stems as supports for their grass nests. Some frog species climb the stems of emergent plants to hunt insects.

A pond can contain many plant types, such as floating plants and emergent plants.

The dry bed of Lake Eyre, in Australia, starts to fill, and birds begin to arrive. Many wetland bird species are waders, which are birds that search for their food in the shallows.

Seasonal wetlands

Many wetlands dry out seasonally, and others are dry most of the time. When it is dry, a wetland can seem a lifeless place, but wetland animals and plants respond quickly when rains or floods come.

Lake Eyre is a 10 000-square-kilometre salt lake in central Australia. It is dry most of the time, but every ten years or so heavy rains swell inland rivers and the lake fills. Within days, billions of brine shrimp hatch from eggs buried in the lakebed. Fish arrive in the floods that come from nearby rivers, and hundreds of thousands of waterbirds arrive from the coast to feed and breed.

Mangrove trees and biodiversity

Mangroves grow in coastal mudflats. When the tide is in, fish search for food among the mangrove roots. When the tide is out, crabs emerge from their burrows to search over the same area. Many fish species breed in the sheltered waters of mangrove forests.

Wetland ecosystems

Living and non-living things, and the **interactions** between them, make up a wetland **ecosystem**. Living things are plants and animals. Non-living things are rocks, soil and water, as well as the **climate**.

Food chains and food webs

A very important way that different **species** interact is by eating or consuming other species. This transfers energy and **nutrients** from one **organism** to another. A food chain illustrates this flow of energy, by showing what eats what. Food chains are best set out in a diagram. A food web shows how many different food chains fit together.

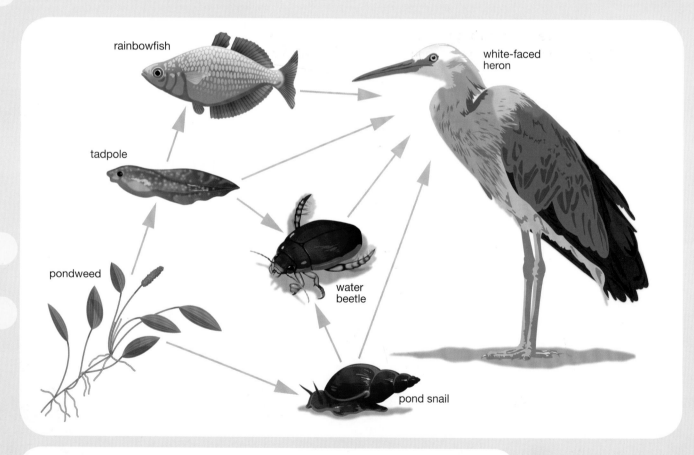

rainbowfish

white-faced heron

tadpole

pondweed

water beetle

pond snail

This wetland food web is made up of several food chains. In one food chain, pondweed is eaten by tadpoles, which are eaten by water beetles, which in turn are eaten by white-faced herons.

Other interactions

Non-living and living things in a wetland **habitat** interact in other ways, too. In eastern Africa, hippopotamuses graze on land during the night and rest in water during the day. While in the water, they release large quantities of dung. The dung provides food for fish and nutrients for **vegetation**.

The breeding of magpie geese in the Kakadu wetlands in northern Australia is linked to the wet and dry seasons. In the wet season, the geese trample the wetland vegetation to make nest platforms that float above the water. These nests are safe from dingoes. The birds' food, wild rice, is also plentiful during the wet season. By the time water levels begin to fall in the dry season, the chicks are ready to fly and can leave the nest.

When hippopotamuses move through a wetland, they create channels as they push aside the vegetation. These channels are new habitats for fish.

Threats to wetlands

Wetlands are under threat from activities such as farming and overfishing. One of the most threatened wetlands is the world's largest freshwater wetland, the Pantanal in South America.

Biodiversity hotspots

There are about 34 biodiversity hotspots in the world. These are regions that have many **endemic species** and where biodiversity is under severe threat from humans. Many include wetlands. The Philippines biodiversity hotspot is home to more than 65 endemic freshwater fish species, many of which are found in one lake only and are at great risk from **invasive species**.

Biodiversity of the Pantanal

The Pantanal is located in western Brazil and reaches into Bolivia and Paraguay. Its biodiversity is very rich because other **habitats**, such as forests and grasslands, are scattered throughout the wetlands. It is on a floodplain that floods each year.

There are known to be 263 fish, 656 bird, 95 mammal, 162 reptile and 40 amphibian species in the Pantanal, and at least 1700 species of flowering plants, not including sedges and grasses. It is one of the last remaining areas where jaguars, pumas, anacondas, giant anteaters, giant river otters and giant armadillos are numerous. There are 500 000 capybaras in the Pantanal. There are also at least 10 million caimans. This is the highest concentration of caimans, crocodiles or alligators in the world.

Giant egrets flock in a wetland in the Philippines. The wetlands in this biodiversity hotspot are under threat.

Threats to Pantanal biodiversity

Part of the Pantanal is protected as a **World Heritage Site**. There are laws to prohibit fishing, **poaching** and illegal logging, but they are hard to enforce in such a large and remote region.

Poaching

Huge profits can be made from poaching. One hyacinth macaw, a large parrot of the Pantanal, can sell for $12 000. Poachers often take the eggs of rare birds and smuggle them abroad, where they are hatched for sale to collectors.

Cattle-grazing

Around 8 million cattle are grazed in the Pantanal. These animals can foul wetlands, trample **vegetation** and destroy habitats.

A giant otter sniffs at a yacare caiman in the Pantanal. Both these species have been threatened by poaching.

Pollution

Gold-mining operations release toxic waste, which finds its way into habitats where it causes loss of biodiversity. Pesticides used on farms also wash into the wetlands, killing fish.

Overfishing

Several fish species are targeted by fishers. Too many fish are caught and some species are threatened with **extinction**.

Did you know?

Since 1800, more than half the world's mangrove forests have been cleared to make way for shrimp farming, roads, ports and other town and tourism developments.

BIODIVERSITY THREAT:
Urbanisation

Wetlands were once regarded as unpleasant places where mosquitoes breed and diseases lurk. Their importance was not understood, so many were drained and filled to make way for roads, houses and ports. **Urbanisation** continues to have a huge effect on wetlands.

Urban pollution

The large number of people in urban areas produces large amounts of pollution. Litter dropped in streets, oil from roads and petrol stations, and household detergents poured down sinks can all be washed into wetlands. Other sources of pollution are chemical leaks from factories and **silt** from building sites. Litter can choke and entangle birds and mammals, chemicals can poison animals, including invertebrate **species**, and silt can smother wetland plants.

There are many dogs in towns and cities, and their faeces carry **nutrients** that cause **algal** blooms, which are toxic and reduce oxygen levels in water. Dog faeces also contain the bacterium *E. coli*, which is harmful to animal health.

Cigarette butts are killers

Cigarette butts are the most numerous item in urban litter. Just one butt contains enough poisons to kill all the microscopic **organisms** in 8 litres of water. If a bird mistakes a butt for food and swallows it, the bird can choke or be poisoned.

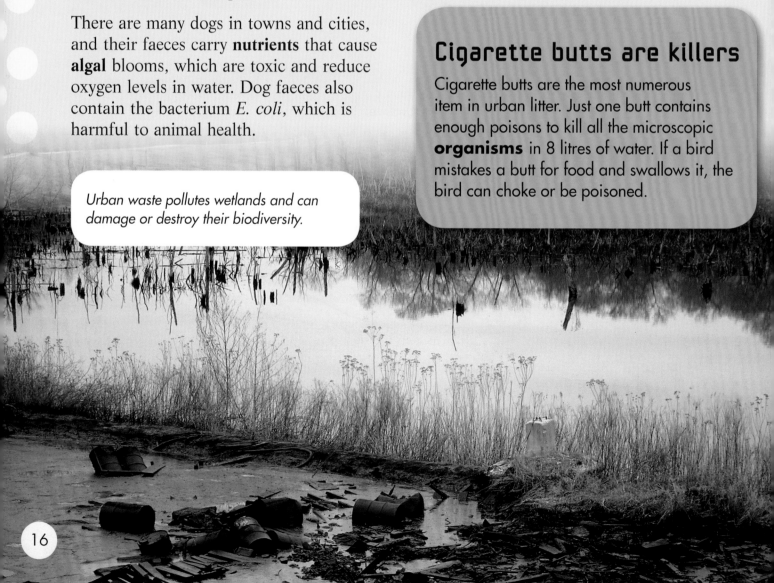

Urban waste pollutes wetlands and can damage or destroy their biodiversity.

The people of cities such as Vancouver, in Canada, appreciate the value of urban wetlands. Many artificial and natural wetlands around the city are protected.

Bioindicators

Bioindicators are organisms that can be used to check the health of an **ecosystem**. Scientists can measure the health of a wetland by observing the type and variety of invertebrates living in it. Some invertebrates, such as mosquitoes, are very tolerant of **pollutants**. Other invertebrates, such as mayflies and mussels, are very sensitive to pollutants. If these sensitive invertebrates are present in a wetland, this indicates that the water is healthy.

Frogs and noise pollution

Male frogs call to female frogs to attract them for mating. A study in Melbourne, in Australia, has shown that city noise makes it harder for frogs to find mates. In a peaceful natural **habitat**, female brown tree frogs can hear the high-pitched call of a male from around 75 metres away. In a city, this distance is reduced to just 20 metres. Frog species that have lower-pitched calls are less affected.

BIODIVERSITY THREAT:
Invasive species

Introduced **species** are non-native species that are introduced into a **habitat** by humans. Some introduced species become **invasive species** and spread widely. They affect local wetland biodiversity in many ways, such as competing with native species for food.

Introducing non-native species

Species may be introduced into a habitat deliberately or accidentally. Asian carp were deliberately introduced into some ponds in North America to help control weeds. When the ponds flooded, the carp entered lake and river systems and became an invasive species.

Introduced snake species in the Everglades

The biodiversity of the Florida Everglades wetlands in the United States is especially threatened by invasive species. Many pet snakes are released into the wetlands when their owners no longer want them. In the ten years up to 2009, more than 1300 introduced snakes were captured in the Everglades. Species included anacondas and boa constrictors from South America and Burmese pythons from south-east Asia. It is likely that for every snake caught, there are hundreds still in the wild. Snakes have few **predators** and they prey heavily on native waterbirds, mammals and fish.

Asian carp can grow up to 120 centimetres long and they eat huge amounts of food. They are invasive species in wetlands in the United States.

Introduced paperbark trees in the Everglades

In the early 1900s, the broad-leaved paperbark tree was introduced to the Everglades as an ornamental tree and to help dry out the wetlands for housing development. This species is native to Australia.

Within a few years, the species had spread widely. No native animals of the Everglades eat the paperbark tree, and so it spreads unchecked. It burns readily, so fire is far more frequent in the Everglades where these plants are found. This kills native plants that are not able to survive fire, and it encourages the growth of even more paperbark trees.

Paperbarks can be chopped down and the stumps can be poisoned, but this is expensive. Scientists have released insects from Australia that eat the paperbark, such as a weevil that eats the leaves and a pysillid, which feeds on the sap. These insects have reduced the spread of the paperbarks, but more insects may be introduced into the Everglades in the future.

Did you know?

The International Union for Conservation of Nature says that where the cause of an animal **extinction** is known, more than 40 per cent of the time it is due to invasive species.

Paperbark is an invasive species that forms dense groups, called stands, where no other plants can grow.

BIODIVERSITY THREAT:
Agriculture

Throughout history, agriculture has been the major cause of wetland loss and degradation. Agricultural chemicals have entered wetlands, poisoning plant and animal **species**. Some wetlands are drained and the land is used for grazing.

Negative effects of agriculture

Agricultural chemicals have the greatest effects on wetland biodiversity. Farmers spread fertilisers on crops and pastures to make them more productive. Some fertiliser is washed from farms into wetlands, causing the quick growth of large amounts of **algae**, called algal blooms. Algae deplete the oxygen in water, killing fish. Pesticides sprayed on crops to kill pests also find their way into wetlands where they can kill both invertebrate and fish species.

Positive effects of agriculture

Not all agricultural activity damages biodiversity. Rice paddies have provided **habitats** for frogs and birds for hundreds of years. In 2005, the 1.5-square-kilometre Kabukuri-numa wetland and surrounding rice paddies in Japan was added to the Ramsar List of Wetlands of International Importance.

Agriculture can have a positive effect on wetland biodiversity. Kabukuri-numa rice paddies in Japan have at least 400 species of plants, 800 species of insects and 32 species of fish, and 200 000 white-fronted geese spend winter there.

Prairie potholes are important habitats for migrating bird species. The prairie pothole region stretches across eight states of the United States.

Prairie potholes

Many shallow wetlands, called prairie potholes, can be found across the prairie grasslands of North America. These potholes were formed by **glaciers** about 12 000 years ago. More than half have been drained for agriculture, which has caused a 50 to 80 per cent fall in the population of wetland birds since 1955.

Since 1985, farmers have been discouraged from draining prairie potholes, and they have been encouraged to return the potholes to their natural state. As a result, waterbird numbers have been increasing. Up to 50 per cent of North America's **migratory** waterbird species depend on prairie potholes as feeding stops.

Did you know?

In the 1600s, the area of land that is now the United States of America (excluding Alaska) probably had around 1 million square kilometres of wetlands. Since then, around 53 per cent has been lost, mainly due to agriculture and **urbanisation**.

BIODIVERSITY THREAT:
Climate change

The world's average temperature is rising because levels of certain gases, such as **carbon dioxide**, are increasing in Earth's atmosphere. These gases, called greenhouse gases, trap heat and cause **climate** change. Climate change affects wetlands in a variety of ways.

Climate change in the past

Climate change is a natural part of Earth's history, and biodiversity has changed as climate has changed. Fossils of obduron, an **aquatic** platypus-like animal, have been found in dry, arid country in eastern Australia. Fifteen million years ago, this area was wetland.

Today, scientists believe the rate of climate change is faster than ever. Effects of climate change could include reduced rainfall and rising temperatures. Scientists think that many **species** will have too little time to **adapt** to climate change and, like obduron, will become **extinct**. However, other species will benefit from climate change and take over the changed **habitats** of extinct species.

River red gums depend on periodic flooding to survive. If climate change reduces the amount of rainfall, there will be fewer floods and the species may die out.

Effects on wetlands

Scientists are uncertain exactly how wetland **ecosystems** will be affected by climate change. They do know that the amount of rainfall and where it falls will change. They also expect sea levels to rise as the polar icecaps melt.

Coastal wetlands

If sea levels rise high enough, coastal wetlands may be destroyed as more salt water enters them. Saltwater animal and plant species will replace freshwater species.

Alpine wetlands

A rise in temperature may lead to groups of alpine animal and plant species becoming separated by warmer valleys. These isolated populations would be at risk, because they cannot breed outside their groups. Through inbreeding, they would lose the **genetic** diversity essential to withstand disease.

Lakes

If a permanent lake begins to dry out for long periods because of lower rainfall, sedges and rushes may be unable to survive. In their place, tree species that are able to tolerate occasional periods of flooding may grow.

Climate change might mean that cold alpine areas become smaller, because snow and ice melts in warmer temperatures. This would reduce the habitat area of alpine wetland species.

Wetland conservation

Conservation is the protection, preservation and wise use of resources and **habitats** such as wetlands. Scientists, governments and local people work together to conserve these habitats.

Research

Research surveys or studies are used to find out information about wetlands, such as how wetland **ecosystems** work and how humans affect them. This information helps people work out ways to conserve wetlands. Researchers may be scientists employed by governments, universities, botanical gardens, zoos or conservation organisations such as Wetlands International.

Breeding programs

Some endangered wetland animals are bred in zoos, where they are safe from threats that could make them **extinct**. In North America, several **species** of salmon are bred in aquariums so that their young can be released into the wild to boost populations.

Community projects

Local community groups can help restore degraded wetlands to their natural state. These groups remove **invasive species** and rubbish, and replant native plants.

Replanting native plant species, both in and out of the water, can help restore and conserve the biodiversity of a wetland.

The Ramsar Convention

Governments around the world have signed an important international agreement for the conservation of wetland biodiversity. This agreement is called the Wetlands of International Importance Convention, but is usually known as the Ramsar Convention. It was first signed by 18 countries in Ramsar, in Iran, in 1971.

By 2010, 159 countries had signed the Ramsar Convention. The Ramsar Convention covers the protection of lakes, rivers, swamps, marshes, wet grasslands, peatlands, oases, **estuaries**, **deltas**, tidal flats, coastal marine areas, mangroves and coral reefs, as well as artificial wetlands such as ponds, rice paddies, reservoirs and salt pans. It lists 1886 wetlands, covering a total area of 1 851 566 square kilometres of wetland habitat, on its list of Wetlands of International Importance.

Migratory birds

Many species of birds **migrate** each year to and from wetlands in different countries. The pectoral sandpiper breeds in the wetlands of Russia and Canada and migrates to the wetlands of Australia and South America for the southern summer. In order to protect these species, each of the countries on the birds' flight path needs to take care of its wetlands.

25

CASE STUDY:
The Okavango Delta

The Okavango Delta is a vast inland wetland within the Kalahari Desert in Botswana. Fed by the Okavango River, the **delta** is home to a spectacular variety of wildlife.

Seasons in the delta

The Okavango Delta varies greatly through the seasons. At the peak of flooding between June and August, the wetland covers around 16 000 square kilometres. It shrinks to 9000 square kilometres over the summer months.

The wet season is during the summer months, from November to March. It is very hot and heavy rain falls in the delta. From March to May, the Okavango River brings the rains that fell 1500 kilometres away in Angola a month or so earlier, and the delta floods. The river water carries around 2 million tonnes of **silt** and **nutrients** that are needed for lush **vegetation** to grow in the delta. This vegetation attracts herbivores such as elephants, impala, lechwe and waterbuck.

The dry season is from April to October, but the height of the flooding happens at this time too, from June to August. The delta dries out and animals gather in huge numbers around the remaining waterholes.

The Okavango Delta is a maze of channels and islands formed by the Okavango River. The river reforms on the other side of the delta and continues to flow through the Kalahari Desert.

Did you know?

High temperatures in the Okavango Delta mean that around 90 per cent of its water is quickly lost to evaporation and transpiration, which is the movement of water through a plant and out through its leaves.

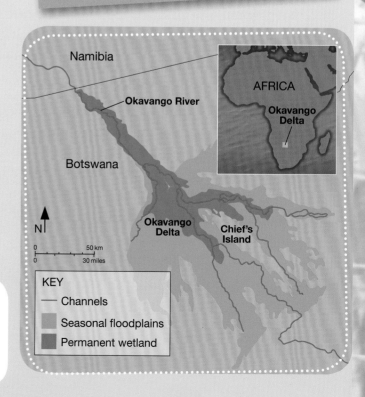

Namibia

Okavango River

AFRICA

Okavango Delta

Botswana

Okavango Delta

Chief's Island

N

0   50 km
0   30 miles

KEY
— Channels
▢ Seasonal floodplains
▢ Permanent wetland

Biodiversity in the delta

The biodiversity of the delta changes with its seasons. Most grazing animals give birth during the wet season, from November to March.

When the delta is flooded, during the dry season, around 200 000 large grazing animals are found in the delta. This is one of the greatest concentrations of grazing animals anywhere in Africa. With so many prey in the delta, **predators** such as lions, hyenas and leopards are also plentiful.

Okavango Delta species

TYPE OF **ORGANISM**	NUMBER OF **SPECIES**
Plants	1300
Birds	444
Mammals	122
Fish	80
Reptiles	64
Amphibians	33

Did you know?

An important feature of the Okavango Delta is Chief's Island. This elevated area of land is 70 kilometres long and 15 kilometres wide. When the waters rise, many of the delta's animals can be found there.

The most common large grazing animal in the Okavango Delta is the lechwe, a type of antelope. It has a population of more than 50 000.

Threats to Okavango biodiversity

Okavango biodiversity is threatened by tourism, **invasive species** and the human population's demand for fresh water.

Tourism

Every year, 120 000 tourists visit the Okavango Delta to see the **delta**'s biodiversity. The tourism industry is very important to Botswana's economy, but it must be properly managed or it can damage the **habitats** that tourists have paid to see. Tourism brings litter and noise, and roads and accommodation need to be built. The local people of the Okavango Delta have complained that tourists leave litter, disturb wildlife and drive their boats over fishing nets. They want all tourists to be accompanied by local guides, to reduce any disturbance to the wetlands.

A local guide takes two tourists through the Okavango Delta. They are travelling in a traditional canoe, called a makoro, which does not disturb wildlife as much as a motorised boat.

Salvinia plants clump together, covering the surface of the water. This weed may have been introduced after aquarium plants were dumped into a river draining into the Okavango. Animals such as elephants can spread the weed as they walk through it.

Salvinia

Salvinia, or kariba weed, is a small floating plant from Brazil that has appeared in the Okavango Delta. Many individual salvinia plants clump together to form huge mats that block light to underwater plants. It can also reduce the oxygen content of the water, causing fish to suffocate and die. A species of weevil that feeds on salvinia has been released into the delta to control the weed. Local communities have been trained to breed and release the weevil. People can also physically remove salvinia mats from the water and burn or compost them.

Demand for water

As human populations grow, the demand for fresh water becomes greater in Botswana, and also in Namibia and Angola, from where the Okavango waters come. The University of Botswana, the Botswana Government, the International Union for Conservation of Nature and the Kalahari Conservation Society are working on a local conservation project in the Okavango Delta. This project aims to ensure that water use, fishing and tourism can continue in ways that do not harm the delta's biodiversity.

What is the future for wetlands?

Many wetlands across the world are still being drained and polluted. However, other wetlands are being restored and new wetlands are being created. Many wetlands are protected by the Ramsar Convention.

What can you do for wetlands?

You can help protect wetlands in several ways.

- Find out about wetlands. Why are they important and what threatens them?
- If you live beside or near a wetland, you can join volunteer groups who replant **vegetation** in wetland areas.
- Become a responsible consumer, and do not litter.
- If you are concerned about wetlands in your area, or beyond, write to or email your local newspaper, your local member of parliament or another politician. Know what you want to say, set out your argument, be sure of your facts and ask for a reply.

Useful websites

🖳 **http://www.ramsar.org**
The Ramsar Convention website explains the aims of this international agreement, lists wetlands of international importance and describes conservation activities and programs.

🖳 **http://www.biodiversityhotspots.org**
This website has information about the richest and most threatened areas of biodiversity on Earth.

🖳 **http://www.iucnredlist.org**
The IUCN Red List has information about threatened plant and animal **species**.

Glossary

adapt   change in order to survive

alga (plural: algae) simple plant without leaves

aquatic   relating to water

brackish   slightly salty, as in a mix of river water and salt water

carbon dioxide   a colourless and odourless gas produced by plants and animals

climate   the weather conditions in a certain region over a long period of time

delta   large area of built-up silt where a river divides before entering the sea

ecosystem   the living and non-living things in a certain area and the interactions between them

endemic species   species found only in a particular area

estuary   sheltered body of water where a river meets the sea

extinct   having no living members

gene   segment of deoxyribonucleic acid (DNA) in the cells of a living thing, which determines characteristics

glacier   river of ice that flows very slowly down a mountain

habitat   place where animals, plants or other living things live

heritage   things we inherit and pass on to following generations

interaction   action that is taken together or actions that affect each other

invasive species   non-native species that spread through habitats

migrate   move from one place to another, especially seasonally

nutrient   chemical that is used by living things for growth

organism   animal, plant and other living thing

poach   illegally hunt or capture wildlife

pollutant   harmful or poisonous human-produced substance that enters an environment, possibly causing damage to organisms

predator   animal that kills and eats other animals

silt   soil and sediments carried in water

species   a group of animals, plants or other living things that share the same characteristics and can breed with one another

urbanisation   the development of towns and cities

vegetation   plants

World Heritage Site   a site that is recognised as having great international importance and that is protected by the United Nations Educational, Scientific and Cultural Organization (UNESCO)

Index